IT'S ABOUT BIRDS

MAY GARELICK
IT'S ABOUT BIRDS

illustrated by TONY CHEN

Holt, Rinehart and Winston
New York

For, lo, the winter is past,
The rain is over and gone;
The flowers appear on the earth;
The time of the singing of birds is come.
From *The Song of Songs*

Text copyright © 1978 by May Garelick
Illustrations © copyright © 1978 by Tony Chen

All rights reserved, including the right to reproduce
this book or portions thereof in any form.
Published simultaneously in Canada by Holt, Rinehart
and Winston of Canada, Limited.

Printed in the United States of America

Library of Congress Cataloging in Publication Data

Garelick, May, 1910–
    It's about birds.

SUMMARY: Describes the characteristics and habits of
birds found in the city, country, and zoo, and at the
beach.
    [1. Birds. 2. Questions and answers] I. Birds—
Juvenile literature. I. Chen, Tony. II. Title.
QL676.2.G37   598.2   77-22712
ISBN 0-03-019431-8

10 9 8 7 6 5 4 3 2 1

List of Illustrations

Before I started to write *It's About Birds,* I talked to an assembly of third, fourth, and fifth graders in a New York City elementary school. Among other things, I told them how I get my ideas for the books I write, and that once I have an idea, I try to find out what children want to know about the particular subject. Then, at the end of my talk, I said I was planning to write a book about birds. Were they interested in birds? They were. Did they have any questions they'd like to ask me about birds? There were so many questions, I couldn't write them fast enough, and I asked the children to write to me. I received seventy-eight letters. Their questions guided me in planning this book.

I would like to thank the children in the third, fourth, and fifth grades of Public School 48 in Brooklyn, New York for their interest and for their help. I especially want to thank Mrs. Clara Kimmelman, Librarian of P. S. 48 for having arranged the assembly and for having sent on the many interesting and useful letters.

About 90 thousand different kinds of birds live in different places in the world.

Except where there are permanent ice caps, where the ice never melts, there is hardly any place on the earth's surface where there are no birds.

This book is only about some of the birds in the world. It's about birds in the city, in the country, at the beach, or in a zoo.

Birds do many incredible things, and this book tells about some of the amazing things they do to survive.

What is a Bird?
Would you say a bird is a creature that flies? But insects fly too, and so do bats, and there are birds that don't fly. Birds have something that no other animal has. Do you know what that is?

13

Feathers. Any animal with feathers is a bird. Feathers are useful in flying, but they are even useful to birds that don't fly. Birds are covered with feathers. Their outer feathers help keep them warm in winter. Watch a bird on a cold day. It looks like a puffball as it fluffs out its feathers to keep out the cold. In summer the flat feathers next to the bird's body help keep it cool. Feathers also keep birds dry in the rain.

Birds take good care of their feathers, bathing them in water or in fine dust. After bathing, they *preen* their feathers. From an oil sac at their tails, they take oil into their beaks and comb it through their

feathers to soften and straighten them. But even with this careful combing and straightening, called *preening,* some feathers get brittle and fall out. Not all at once, just one or two at a time. As they fall out, new feathers grow in.

If you find one of these feathers, put a drop of water on it and watch the water slide off. Try to break or tear it, and you'll see how strong it is.

Birds Eat Different Foods

What does a bird do most of the time? It eats. And when it is not eating, it is looking for food. Flying from tree to tree to tree to peck at berries and fruit, digging in the ground for seeds and worms, diving for fish, flying after insects, hunting small animals —eating and searching for food are how birds spend most of the day.

Birds Live Where Food is Plentiful

Different birds eat different foods, so they live where they can find their food. Birds that eat seeds and grasses, nuts and berries, live where these foods grow. Birds that eat worms, caterpillars, and insects live in places where these are plentiful. Birds that live on fish or water plants live near water. Birds that make a meal of mice, snakes, or other small animals live where they can hunt them. Some birds, like crows, can live anywhere. Crows can dig up newly planted corn in the spring, eat ripe corn in summer, and capture young mice in their nests. Crows eat all kinds of food, even dead, smelly animals, so they can live anywhere.

This *protective* coloring helps birds to survive. It helps to protect them from *predators*—animals that hunt.

Male and female birds often look alike, equally bright or dull. But in many *species*—kinds—the male is more colorful than the female. The male cardinal is bright red. The female is reddish-brown. You can tell a male mallard from a female. His head is bright green, while the female is all brown.

Since it's the female that mostly sits on the eggs and takes care of the baby birds, her dull color protects the nest from enemy birds.

Besides the difference in the color of birds, there's also the difference in size.

How Big Are Birds?
The beautiful Bee Hummingbird is actually this size. It is the smallest bird in the world. It weighs less than a penny. You could hold one in your hand if you could ever catch it. But the hummingbird would be hard to catch. It never seems to stop moving. It even flies backwards. It flies from flower to flower looking for *nectar*—the juice inside flowers. Even while it sucks the nectar from the flowers, it is always moving. Its tiny wings beat back and forth so fast you can hardly see them. In one second, as long as it takes you to say one-two-three, the hummingbird beats its wings seventy-five times. This whirring wingbeat makes a humming sound, which is how the hummingbird got its name.

The tallest bird in the world is the ostrich. It is taller than the tallest basketball player. A person as tall as an ostrich would be a giant. The tall ostrich weighs about 300 pounds.

Some Birds Don't Fly

From the smallest to the tallest, all birds have feathers, and all birds have wings. But they don't all fly. Then why do we say "fly like a bird"? Because most birds do fly. But some don't.

The ostrich is a grass-eating bird. It doesn't have to fly around to find its food. The grass is right there, where the ostrich is.

Look how little its wings are. They are much too small to lift this big bird into the air. So the ostrich can't fly, and it doesn't need to but it can run very fast.

Chickens on a farm don't fly around for their food either. The farmer tosses out corn and other seeds, and all the chickens have to do is peck on the ground for their food. Sometimes you may see a chicken get off the ground, but its wings are too small to lift it high enough for flying.

Penguins also don't need to fly. Their food, fish, is in the water. To get to the water they walk. But often there is ice and snow in the land of the penguins, and it is slippery for walking. So they slide to the water on their stomachs. Their small wings that look like flippers help penguins keep their balance while sliding and also help them swim. While swimming, they use their webbed feet for steering and stopping.

Small birds, tall birds, birds that fly, and birds that don't fly all have ways of getting their food. They all have beaks.

Birds Have Different Beaks

Some beaks are short, some are long, some bent, some hooked. Some beaks are spearlike, others are spoonlike. Some are upturned, others downturned, some are crossed.

The pointed beaks of cardinals and sparrows are shaped to pick up and crack open tiny seeds. Robins with their longer beaks can dig into the ground for worms.

A strong, hooked beak for tearing up captured animals is the beak of an owl, a hawk, an eagle, or any bird of *prey,* that feeds on animals.

Many water birds use their beaks to scoop food out of the water. Some of these birds have ridges inside their wide, flat beaks. These ridges are strainers. They strain out the water and leave insects, small fish, or water plants, which the birds then swallow.

26

Birds have no teeth. Their beaks are their teeth, their nutcrackers, or traps for catching insects and water plants. With their beaks, birds get their food, bite it, grind it, or tear it apart.

Legs, Feet, and Beaks Help Birds Get Food
By looking at a bird's beak you can often tell what kind of food it eats. Besides beaks, birds often use their legs and feet to help them get their food. For example, the sharp claws of a woodpecker help him up a tree. He climbs up and clings to the tree trunk with his claws. With his beak, he taps at the bark to disturb the insects underneath. When the insects start moving, the woodpecker sees or hears them and snaps them up with his long pointed beak. Woodpeckers also use their beaks to drill, crack, and hammer at nuts to open them.

Some water birds use their feet to dig up shellfish at the beach. A seagull looks for a clam, and flies up from the beach, holding the clam in its beak. From up in the air, the seagull drops the clam on the soft sand at the edge of the water. The clam shell doesn't break open. Still, that gull will drop that clam over and over again in the soft sand to try to break it open. Finally, he flies off with the clam in his beak, probably to find some hard ground or rock on which to crack the shell.

The kingfisher is a bird that eats fish. Since it doesn't have webbed feet, it cannot swim to get its food. Instead, the kingfisher flies to a tree by the water, clamps its feet over a branch, and waits until it sees a fish. Then it dives down and catches the fish in its long, pointed beak.

Herons eat fish, too. They don't have webbed feet either and don't swim. But the heron's legs are long enough for wading. The heron stands and waits at the edge of the water. When it sees a fish or a frog, it wades into the water and seizes it in its long, pointed beak.

Birds use their beaks and feet for more than eating. Can you guess for what?

Building Nests

Beaks are their hands and their tools for building nests. With their beaks and their feet, they gather, carry, and weave together the materials used to build nests.

Each type of bird builds its own special kind of nest. No two species build exactly the same style nest. People who study and know about birds can often tell the kind of bird by its nest.

All American robins, no matter where they live, build their nests the same way. A nest made of woven twigs and grasses, and lined with mud, is a robin's nest. Sometimes, robins build their nests on protected window sills, but mostly their nests are in trees.

In the spring, before the time comes for the female robin to lay her eggs, she starts the nest. The male robin helps her gather twigs and grasses and helps her carry in some mud. The nest is woven, lined with mud, and the female robin turns around in the mud until the nest is shaped like a bowl. When the mud is smooth and dry, she lines it with soft grasses.

With its beak, the Tailor Bird punctures holes around the edges of leaves. Then she sews the leaves together with plant threads, ties the knots, and builds her nest inside these leaves. You can see why this bird is called a Tailor Bird.

A woodpecker pecks away at the bark of a tree with her beak. She drills and digs into the bark until she scoops out a nest that will be safe for her eggs and her babies.

The song sparrow builds her nest on the ground, hidden under weeds and stalks. Her eggs are the color of the ground and dry grass. Here her eggs and babies will have a chance to be safe from cats or other prowlers.

The little hummingbird builds a tiny cup of a nest, just big enough for two little eggs, each about the size of a pea. The mother bird wraps silky plant threads around her beak which she weaves into her nest.

If you see a deep sack hanging from a high branch in a tall tree, it's probably the nest of an oriole. With her beak and feet, the oriole weaves loops of string and plant fibers around the forked twigs of a tree. Inside the nest she adds things she has found on the ground, such as bits of wool and plant *down*—fine, soft seeds like dandelion fluff. Wherever there are orioles there are nests like this.

Each species of bird, no matter where it lives, builds its nest the way its parents did. The parents don't have to teach them how to build a nest. Birds just naturally know how.

When you just naturally know how to do something, without having to learn about it, it is called *instinct*. Birds are born with this instinct. They will build their own kind of nest even if they have never seen a nest built before.

Some Birds Don't Build Their Own Nests
Some birds use the nests that other birds made. The little Elf Owl's nest in a cactus plant in the desert was drilled by a woodpecker. A woodpecker drilled into the tough shell of the cactus to make its nest. After the young woodpeckers were old enough to leave the nest, the Elf Owl moved in.

Cowbirds and certain cuckoos lay their eggs in other birds' nests. They leave their eggs to be *incubated*—hatched—by "foster" parents. When the eggs hatch, the foster parents feed the baby cowbirds or cuckoos.

Some Birds Don't Have Nests
In the Antarctic, where no nesting material is available, the male penguin carries the single egg, which the female penguin lays, in a warm fold on top of his foot. The egg is kept safe and warm there for two months, until the chick is ready to hatch.

Shore birds, like gulls and terns, lay their eggs on the bare sand. Sometimes they put pebbles or shells around the eggs, perhaps to protect them.

No matter what kind of nest they build, or where it is—on the ground, in a tree, on a window sill—or

even if they build no nest at all, birds lay their eggs near food and water, where they will be safe, protected from bad weather and from enemy birds. There the babies, when hatched, will be safe and protected.

In the spring you can see birds gather material for nest building. A robin may fly by with a twig in its beak. An oriole may be carrying a piece of string to weave into her nest. If you leave some wool or string on the ground, a bird may come to pick it up. If you see any soft, downy feathers on the ground, you'll see birds come to collect them for lining their nests.

Birds whose nests are in the hole of a tree will often use the same nest again. But other birds build new nests each spring. For them, a nest is not a home to come back to. It's a cradle for their babies to be hatched in and to grow up in.

How Long Does it Take to Build a Nest?
If the weather is good and there is no rain, it takes a bird about a week to build a nest. A day or so later, the mother lays the first egg. Most birds lay one egg a day. Some birds lay only one or two eggs; most birds lay about four or five eggs and some lay as many as twenty eggs.

When the eggs are laid, the mother bird sits on the whole *clutch*—all the eggs—to keep them warm. She incubates them. She turns them regularly. The eggs must be kept warm so the babies inside the shells can grow. But she can't sit on the eggs all the time. She must eat. Some birds cover their eggs with leaves to keep them warm and protected from enemy birds that might eat them. When the nest is protected, the mother bird can fly off to get some food. Sometimes the father bird sits on the eggs while the mother leaves the nest to feed herself. And some father birds bring food to the mother.

How Long Does it Take for the Babies to Hatch?

Within a few weeks, a little tapping sound comes from inside one of the eggs. A chick is getting ready to hatch out of the shell. With a sharp point near the end of its beak, called the *egg tooth,* the chick taps from inside the shell. It *pips* at the shell. Little by little, in a few hours or perhaps as long as a whole day, the babies break out of their shells. The mother takes the empty shells in her beak, throws them out of the nest, or carries them away from the nest. She doesn't want enemy birds to know that her chicks have hatched.

Then she snuggles her wet chicks—she *broods* them. She covers them with her body to keep them warm and safe from bad weather or from enemy birds.

Feeding the Babies

Some birds are born naked with no feathers. Some hatch with a light covering of soft down feathers. They can't see. Soon after they hatch, their beaks open wide for food. Baby birds are always hungry. Their parents are busy the whole day long, feeding themselves and their helpless babies—the *nestlings.* When the parent bird returns with the food, the chicks can feel the nest shake. The hungry nestlings

jostle one another, raising their beaks and peeping. The nestlings *gape*—open their mouths wide—and the mother pushes the food down into the babies' throats. Sometimes the father brings food to the nest, puts it in the mother's beak, and she stuffs it deep into the babies' throats.

For the first few days, young birds, even those that will grow to be seed-eaters, are fed insects and small worms.

All day long the babies are fed. They grow bigger. They grow stronger. In a few days their feathers begin to grow. Their eyes begin to open. Soon they can see.

When they have all their feathers, they will be able to leave the nest.

The Fledglings Leave the Nest
Days before they are ready to leave the nest, the *fledglings*—young birds learning to fly—get restless. They push, peck, and jostle one another in the crowded nest. They flap their wings and seem to be interested in things outside the nest. Sometimes they snap at insects that fly by.

Although they all seem eager to leave the nest, they leave one at a time. Often the first bird leaving is a signal for the others to follow.

Sometimes a fledgling hesitates, and the mother may have to coax it out of the nest with some food. She may hold a worm in her beak for the baby bird to see. She flies to a branch close by. The young bird, now almost as big as the parent, rises from the nest and flies out to get the worm.

Day by day their flying muscles grow stronger. In a few days they will be strong enough to start looking for food.

Are the Young Birds on Their Own Now?
Not yet. They still need help and protection, and their parents usually take care of them until they can take care of themselves.

Parent birds have different warning cries, and their young recognize these warnings. When they hear the familiar warning, they fly away or crouch and hide until the enemy leaves.

As the young birds grow, they learn to protect themselves. If a cat, a dog, or a person comes prowling around, a bird can fly up to a tree and escape. But suppose the enemy is another bird, a bigger bird?

Protecting Themselves from Enemies
Different birds have different ways of protecting themselves. The little desert Elf Owl has a trick of "freezing" and playing dead until the enemy leaves. Other birds use this freezing trick in times of danger.

Crows post guards to be on the lookout while the other crows are eating. If an enemy owl, hawk, or eagle flies by, the guards start cawing, calling, and squawking. When the others hear the alarm call, they fly to safety.

Owls and some other birds have a way of raising their feathers to puff themselves out and look twice their size. They look so ferocious, the attacking bird is frightened off.

The big ostrich, which can run faster than a horse but can't fly, has a trick of hiding its head on the ground. Upended this way, it looks like a bush and often fools the enemy. If the enemy is not fooled, a sudden kick from an ostrich is enough to send him on his way.

How and Where Do Birds Sleep?

In choosing a nightly *roost*—a place to sleep—many birds choose the kind of place they were born in. Those born in forests fly to a tree in the forest, clasp their claws around a branch, and go to sleep. When a bird lets its weight down, the muscles of its feet tighten, and no matter how soundly it sleeps, its feet are locked so tightly around the branch that its grip never loosens. Most birds sleep with their beaks tucked in their feathers.

Some birds sleep in bushes, some on the ground, and seabirds sleep on or near the water.

Some birds sleep singly, some in pairs, and some in family groups. The Bobwhite family sleeps in a tight circle with all heads pointing out. Their back feathers are the color of the earth, pebbles, and leaves and help *camouflage*—hide—them from enemies. Should danger threaten, they can fly out of the circle without bumping into one another.

Wherever birds sleep, and however they sleep, birds choose a roost where they will be safe from animals that prowl at night.

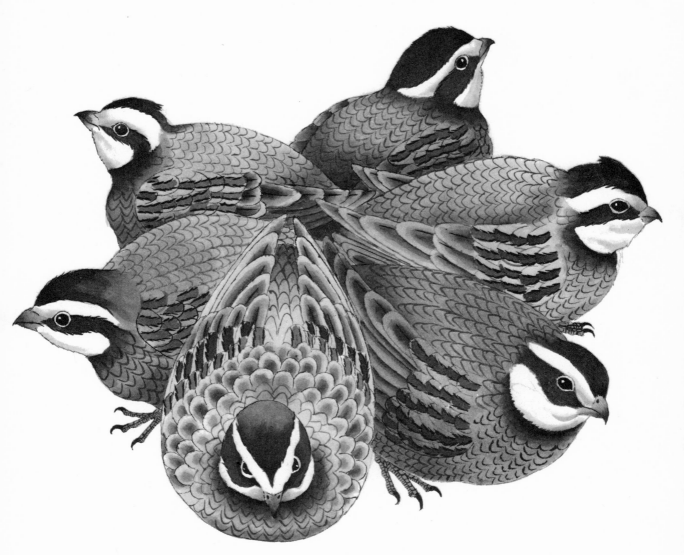

As it gets later in the day, you hear fewer and fewer birds. After dark you may hear the hoot of an owl, the call of a mockingbird. But most birds are asleep. Most birds have exact times for going to roost at night, and they have definite waking hours. Robins are among the earliest to awaken, while blue jays are late risers.

Birds Migrate For the Winter

It is late summer. All the baby birds are full grown. The parent birds have raised their families. There are more birds now than there were in the spring. The leaves begin to turn color. There are fewer flies, not so many mosquitoes. Bugs and bees will disappear. Frost will kill some insects, and some insects will sleep for the winter under stones or in tree barks until warm weather comes again.

The days grow shorter. There's less time for birds to hunt for food. Food is becoming scarce.

Birds begin to gather in flocks. They're getting ready to *migrate*—travel—to where the days are longer and food is more plentiful. They will spend the winter far from home, far from where they were raised.

How Do Birds Know When to Leave Home?

People have been studying this question for a long time. Some say birds leave to escape bad weather, others say to find food. But they leave in summer when food is still available and cold weather has not yet come. We don't really know why birds leave when they do.

How Do They Travel?

Some birds migrate alone and keep in touch with other birds by frequent calls. But traveling in flocks helps birds *forage*—look—for food and escape enemies. Some families migrate together, the older birds guiding the young to the place where they wintered the year before. But many migrant birds that were hatched in the spring and have never made such a trip seem to know when, where, and how to travel, without being guided by older birds.

Traveling by day and at night, some flying thousands of miles over oceans, deserts, and mountains, they stop often to feed. Some birds, particularly the smaller ones, migrate at night and feed and rest during the day. But swallows and swifts that catch insects while flying migrate by day when insects are easy to see.

49

How Do Birds Find Their Way?

We don't know yet. There are different ideas. Some people say they are guided by stars, some say by instinct. Many people are working to understand the mystery of migration. In past years, thousands of birds have been *banded.* A small, numbered aluminum band is put around the bird's leg. The bird scientist keeps a record—of the numbers, the kind of bird it is, when it leaves, and from where it leaves. When the bird arrives at its winter home, the aluminum band is checked. This is how people have found out where birds spend the winter and how long it takes them to get there.

Some Birds Do Not Migrate

Blue jays, White-breasted Nuthatches, little Black-capped Chickadees, cardinals, and Downy Woodpeckers stay close to their breeding places all winter. They feed on available food, boring into trees for beetles and grubs, finding acorns and seeds in dry grasses and weeds. Birds that don't migrate for the winter have to work hard to get the food they need. So people help. They put out bird seed and *suet*— which is fat.

How Do Birds Find Their Way Back Home?
We don't know this either. The aluminum bands help us to find out. By checking the bands of the returning birds, people found out that a bird migrating from its summer home comes back to that same territory. A robin from Maine comes back to its home state. How birds find their way back is still a mystery. But as nice as it is for birds in their winter homes, they return to their summer homes in the spring. The summer home is a bird's real home. Here it was hatched, and here it will raise its family.

From the first week in March to the end of May, thousands of birds are on their way back to their real homes.

Swifts, the fastest flying birds (that's how they got their name), fly more than 100 miles an hour. But robins and blackbirds are the first birds to return in the spring.

The days are warmer. The birds are back. The air is alive with their songs and calls.

What Do the Different Sounds Mean?
When the mother hen clucks, she may be calling her chicks to come along. Her chicks follow. Ducklings

follow their quacking mother. Maybe she's telling them that food is near, and that they should come and get it.

An alarm call warns other birds to watch out. A sharp warning call may mean that there is a hawk overhead and the birds should take care.

Why Do Birds Sing?

Each species has its own songs, its own calls, its special song to attract a mate. If you hear a pigeon cooing and gurgling, over and over again, that pigeon is probably looking for a mate.

Mostly it's the male bird that sings. Some birds have several songs. They may be songs of joy, or a song might mean: I claim this tree. It's mine. Keep out. Another song might mean: I'm a robin, here in this tree. Where are you? A female robin calls back. She may be calling, I'm here. The male robin sings back. He may be singing, Come be with me.

Soon they will build their nest. The female will lay her eggs. The chicks will hatch out. The parent birds will feed them and care for them until they can fly and feed themselves. All summer long young birds will be flying, eating, and calling. Then, in early fall, they will begin to gather in flocks, getting ready to migrate to their winter feeding grounds, leaving be-hind the cardinals, blue jays, chickadees and other birds that spend their winters and summers in the same place.

But the migrants will come back next spring as they have come back every spring.

54

Were There Always Birds?
Long before there were people on earth, when there were dinosaurs, there were also birds. Then, millions of years ago, birds were different from the birds we see today.

Birds that didn't develop useful beaks, powerful claws, and strong flight feathers became *extinct*— they're no longer around. Many birds became extinct because they were unable to fly to more plentiful feeding grounds or to escape their enemies.

How Birds Survive

The birds we see today have developed ways to stay alive. Without rakes, tractors, or fishing rods they get their food. With built-in tools they build their nests. Without maps or compasses they travel hundreds of miles, over land and water, to new feeding grounds and find their way back to their original home territory, where they raise their families. There they feed and protect their babies that grow to have families of their own. This is how birds survive and stay alive. But birds don't live alone in the world.

Are Birds Safe Now?

Over the years people and other animals have hunted birds for food. Their eggs have been taken from their nests. Their colorful feathers have been used to beautify hats and clothes, their soft feathers to make pillows. As the country grew, forests were bulldozed and farms torn down to make room for homes and roads. Many swamps where birds nested were drained, and birds were crowded out of their feeding and nesting homes. Then came the use of insecticides that killed the insects that some birds ate, and more and more birds were in danger of becoming extinct.

People decided that the time had come to do something for the *endangered species*—birds that were in danger of being killed off. Laws were passed and land set aside where birds would be safe.

Will There Always Be Birds?
Now, all over the country, in national and state parks there are wildlife *sanctuaries*—shelters where birds are protected from danger—where they can feed, nest, and raise their young. There are even special islands reserved for birds.

Now, armed with binoculars and cameras, but without guns, in every part of the country, in summer or winter, in fair or rainy weather, from dawn to dark, and even in the middle of the night, people visit woods, forests, and parks to watch, to listen, and to enjoy the wonder of the birds.

Index with Identification Hints *

About the Author

MAY GARELICK was born in Russia but was brought to the U.S. before she was one year old. During her childhood she developed a life-long love for the country and nature and with it a keen sense of observation. Recently, while giving a talk to third, fourth and fifth graders, she told them she was planning to write a book about birds and asked them to write her with their questions. She received 78 letters with hundreds of questions which served as a guide for writing this book.

Ms. Garelick lives in New York City where she works as an author and free-lance editor. She has written many books for children, among them *Where Does the Butterfly Go When It Rains, What's Inside the Egg, Down to the Beach* and *About Owls,* an ALA Notable Book for 1975.

About the Artist

TONY CHEN, an art director for *Newsweek* magazine, is also a painter and sculptor. Many of his paintings, watercolors and pieces of sculpture are in private collections.

A *cum laude* graduate of the Pratt Institute, he has illustrated a number of children's books, among them *Too Many Crackers* and *About Owls.* He lives with his wife and two sons on Long Island.